Get Powerful Now

get POWERFUL NOW!

Your Guide to Moving On

CAROL ZURITA

NEW YORK

LONDON • NASHVILLE • MELBOURNE • VANCOUVER

Get Powerful Now

Your Guide to Moving On

Published in New York, New York, by Morgan James Publishing. Morgan James is a trademark of Morgan James, LLC. www.MorganJamesPublishing.com

ISBN 9781642790368 paperback
ISBN 9781642790177 eBook
Library of Congress Control Number: 2018936416

Cover Design by:
Megan Dillon
megan@creativeninjadesigns.com

Interior Design by:
Chris Treccani
www.3dogcreative.net

Morgan James is a proud partner of Habitat for Humanity Peninsula and Greater Williamsburg. Partners in building since 2006.

Get involved today! Visit
MorganJamesPublishing.com/giving-back

For all the super women out there who found their life purpose. Also, for the ones who are still searching for it. Keep the strength and the faith. You'll get there!

This one was originally written with the intention of reminding myself about that strength I once grew. Although, this is just a chapter in my life; it is not the end. So, I may need to come back and reuse these steps for myself.

For my dearest readers, I offer the same suggestion to use this guide more than once not only during the thunderstorm but also during the summers in your life.

I intend to express my true love and gratitude…

To my beautiful blended family, who is just the best blessing given.

To Djamel Elgarni: thank you for being what I needed to become a woman.

To the ladies and guy who were my companions during this episode–Henar Cano, Antonia Sedova, Meir Simhi, Anastasia Button, and Eliana Salter–I cherish your friendship.

Also, my deepest appreciation to Dustin Watchman for helping me find the best publisher.

And to Patrick Schmidt for the support that made this one a published book, at last.

Contents

INTRODUCTION

Cinderella, Snow White, Rapunzel, and the rest of the Disney princesses—whose lives all ended happily with the most charming princes in town—were the bedtime stories for my female friends and me. Our parents did not know how dangerous these tales were.

Grown girls may wait for days, months, or perhaps years for that man who is supposed to be their support, guard, refuge, provider, romantic, and forever-loyal partner called "the other half." And not only that, but we believe in the "happily ever after" only after our prince charming arrives.

That makes us assume we are not a whole, but a half, and they are the other half we need to feel complete.

However, this belief is not forever. A bad breakup or disappointment shakes us and wakes us up from that innocent yet silly fairy tale.

Society tells us the first kiss is unforgettable and forever magical. I disagree. I understand that the chemical change that happens within the body of a teenager is unique. Every emotion is felt with greater intensity than it is in an adult's body, so the initial feeling might be felt as sweet. But as my grandma always says, there are two sides of the coin. Here is the other side of mine: When I think of my first kiss, I become disgusted and it only gets worse.

Right after turning fifteen during the summer of 2001, I decided to spend more time with the girls who had the most male friends so I could experience what they all talked about… boys.

On most days we would be done with school by 1:15 p.m. My school was for girls only, so by the end of the morning boys from other neighboring schools with different uniforms and funny hairstyles had packed the outside of our building. To most of the female students, the fun was always on the other side of the school walls.

One sunny day while we packed our books and got ready to walk out the school's gate, one of my girlfriends told me she had arranged for a male friend of her boyfriend's to join us while we all walked towards the bus station to go home. Although my bus station was three minutes from the school, I sometimes made the fifteen-minute walk with them to their bus station so I could stick around and not miss the fun.

During the walk, I was naïve but curious. My hands were sweaty, and I wondered how my hair looked in the humid air. (Even in my thirties I still can't keep my thick and long hair looking decent.) Right across the street, a pack of six boys tried to look cool and pretended to be all grown up.

The other five girls and I were walking towards them from the other side of the road. The girls kissed their boyfriends' lips, and I noticed there was this new boy whom no one was kissing. My friend Alexandra didn't forget the mission. She grabbed my arm, walked me towards this tanned guy, and introduced me to him.

"Carol, meet my good friend, Oscar," she said. "Oscar, this is Carol. She also lives in the South. She is walking with us to the bus stop."

I was confused. Should I smile much? I mean, he may think I am "too easy."

Should I stay serious? But he may get scared of me…

The vibe I got from him was…okay. Not that much excitement but nothing against him either.

We had hung out for about two weeks or so when the girls told me Oscar liked me. I expected a much more handsome guy for me.

At that time, my insecurities always made decisions for me.

Was I pretty enough to get a good-looking guy? Maybe this was all I could get. That was always the internal fight.

Another school day was done, and I began the usual routine of walking with the same group towards the bus stop. Oscar grabbed my arm and tenderly pulled me closer to him. He tried to sound and look as gentlemanly as possible. He told me he liked me and asked if I would like to be his girlfriend. I did not reply with a firm "yes," but instead played with words and made silly comments like, "We live far away from each other, so this commitment may not work." I also said that Mom didn't allow me to go out on the weekends like other girls' moms.

And at the end I said that if he accepted those facts I may think about his proposition. I didn't want to say *yes* but I didn't want to say *no* either.

He didn't say much but took my hand and walked me a couple of blocks away. To my surprise, he told the group he'd take me home, so we took a different way. A few minutes later, the bus arrived and we stepped on. He sat beside me and suddenly leaned over me, and with the best intentions of making the moment romantic, he put his lips on mine. I did not expect that to happen, so with my lips closed, he just stuck his tongue on me... *Yuck!* I thought.

He was the first in a queue of other guys who walked in and out of my life over the next ten years.

The Beginning

In my early twenties, I found that when I looked at my high school classmates' posts on social media and their "happy ever after" pictures of their weddings and children, I felt sorry for myself.

I could replay those constant moments like an old movie tape and felt as though I was the last one at everything. At the age of twelve, the girls I hung out with shared experiences about their first period. This was another topic they had in common that excluded me because mine arrived many months after theirs. Then all the girls had their first "real" French kiss at the age of fourteen, while I choked at the first trial one a year after.

Most girls already knew how fun it was to sneak into a bar with a fake ID, get drunk, and buy cigarettes while they were underage. But my single mother would never let me leave home to hang out with friends before my eighteenth birthday. So I got to learn about bars and other nighttime activities long after everyone else.

"Why am I the one who experiences everything last?" I constantly cried. "Is it true that good things come to those who wait?"

As I wrote about these memories I wondered what it would be like if humans got everything they craved right away. Would it be messier than what it usually is? I don't mean to sound negative, but life is hard sometimes and you all know about that. One gets to understand the *why* of patience when wisdom comes in the thirties. Perhaps if I got everything I wanted immediately it may not be what I expected.

I wasn't experienced in relationships and years later endured several breakups and disappointments. I lived the only relationship I knew over and over again with different men.

I was tired of this routine and thought if I ran away I would experience something different. I assumed I was not the only one who went to bed every night who thought, *I wish I could be far away from this mess.*

I actually did move to the other side of the world and expected the pain and sorrow to stop.

I landed in China in early 2012 and met people from different backgrounds and learned about cultures, language, food, and, of course, dating.

Modern music beat loudly in every smoky bar in town. I ventured out night after night to celebrate the freedom and the distance between me and the roller coaster of emotions I had felt years back.

Without much thought I had little crushes, flames, and adventures with men from various nationalities. It was fun to describe myself as the "perfect Latin woman" and continue the quest of "What's up! Where're you from?" But despite the experience, after a few months it bothered me again.

I was back to square one. Loneliness and regret resurfaced, and the desire to find "my other half" came back.

An advertisement for a popular brand of body wash placed two basic labels at the top of two side-by-side gates to demonstrate how weak self-love can be. One of the labels was "Beautiful" while the other one was "Average." Researchers observed the choices women made. Some who felt very confident chose the "beautiful" one, while others hesitated or changed their choice to the "average" one.

When the ladies were asked about their decisions, the ones who chose the "beautiful" gate said they never hesitated about their looks and whole self. The other group of women who chose the "average" gate couldn't explain why they felt that way about their looks. They thought they weren't attractive enough to be called beautiful.

Some years back, the audiobook *You Can Heal Your Life* by Louise Hay was the first lesson that taught me a new understanding of self-love and self-appreciation. I not only gained confidence towards myself, but I also gained an abundance of time, energy, and wealth when I practiced her words of wisdom.

I repeated affirmations, mantras, and visualizations for many hours to attract what I thought would make me happy, and it worked perfectly.

I remember the visualization map my elder sister and I made on December 31, 2010. We collected some magazines and newspapers and made sure they were old enough so we wouldn't make Mom angry. She said she needed the current paper to read whenever she had time, although she never did.

We cut out pictures of beautiful locations in the world where we could travel to and perhaps live. I paid a lot of attention to the graphics of couples and their postures and hoped one day I could find a similar love for which I starved the most.

I was very young and wanted to be loved. However, I preferred to avoid images of couples getting married because I didn't like the way marriage was modeled in my life. My grandparents' marriage, as well as Mom's first and second marriages, weren't the example of happy-ever-after relationships.

I was not sure about getting married someday—especially when the number of my breakups equaled the number of pairs of shoes I owned. Like a lot of girls, I had a unique pair of shoes for almost each of my outfits.

Other pictures in the magazines and newspapers showed wide, glass windows with the sea in sight and tons of expensive outfits, both of which were also on my map.

I guess I did a fantastic job of looking up at my vision board every day when I woke up and before I went to sleep, because everything that was on the board *happened indeed!* Yes, I had it all two years later.

That picture of the perfect man in a perfect couple became a reality too. I was sure that the relationship I had stared at for about 1,460 times within two years would be mine when I met a French man in a bar one evening.

That warm autumn evening, after I returned from work with a lot on my mind, I thought it would help me relax if I went out and enjoyed the night. I put on a silly black top that didn't suit me well and a cheap gray skirt. I pulled my hair up in a ponytail, added more mascara, and put on some red lipstick. I took just twenty-five *kuai* (Chinese currency) with me and went to the street and stopped a moto taxi, which dropped me off at the most popular party place in Shekou, just ten minutes away.

It was Wednesday, my favorite day. The bar was usually only full on weekends. That night I did not expect to meet the love of my life in a fairly empty place, although I may have wished for that to happen.

The Terrace bar is very well known on *TripAdvisor*, not only because of the great food, but also because of the live Filipino band that plays seven days a week.

I sat in a very strategic place behind a wooden column at the large tiled bar, with a full pack of cigarettes in hand. I didn't feel attractive and was shy for being alone, so I kept myself away from the little crowd to enjoy the music.

I lit one cigarette after another and noticed a couple of business guys step in. They sat across the bar where they had a wide view of me. I quickly moved my eyes to spy on them a couple of times. I saw a smile on one of their faces.

The waiter approached me and asked what nationality I was. I said, "South American."

He offered me another drink and handed me one of his cigarettes—which is normal in Chinese culture. He was in the middle at the round bar and served me on one side and the businessmen on the other side. One of the mature visitors from the opposite side came over and stood behind me to break the ice. He was a good-looking French guy.

He said, "The bartender told me you were from South Africa. I moved to your side to prove he was wrong because you look anything but South African." We both laughed. China is so far away from my hometown that its people have a hard time identifying South Africans and South Americans.

We shared drinks and dances together and made out on the dance floor a few times before we ended up in my apartment.

I liked him; he liked me!

We had a few dates on the phone during his long business trip a few months later. Once his trip ended, neither of us hesitated to live together as a real and loving couple.

It was the first time I shared my daily routine with a man. I was agitated, fearful, and excited all at the same time. Eventually, everything settled down and friends and family noticed how well the two of us got along. There were different family portraits of him and me on Christmas and at birthday parties in every closest friend's camera.

We had a fun routine day after day. We woke up early each morning, had breakfast, rushed to work, returned home after seven to make dinner, did the dishes and sometimes laundry, and waited for Friday. Our perfect routine was parties with friends and lazy Sundays.

I was so confident and proud of the love I had for this man. I wanted to dedicate the rest of my youth and maturity to him with my whole being. I was his and he was mine!

This relationship was as good as creamy vanilla ice cream. I never got tired of it. He was wise, mature, generous, spiritual, caring, hilarious, and most importantly in love with me. *Yes, charming princes do really exist, as well as happy endings,* I thought multiple times within the next twenty months of happiness. Then the unexpected happened.

Black Sunday

One Thursday in May, I woke up in the middle of the night from an awful nightmare. I dreamed that someone was warning me about Grandpa's unexpected death, and the tragedy felt so real that my heart ached and I stopped breathing for a few seconds. I panted but was determined to escape from the nightmare. I forced myself to open my eyes, and nonstop tears followed.

But it wasn't about Grandpa. Although I was not sure what was about to happen, my sixth sense knew something was wrong between my man and me.

A few days prior to this, there was tension between the two of us. In my mind it was just something couples go through, but in my chest it felt like we were not "us" anymore; rather, it was "you and me." Pain and loneliness invaded and made things worse when one Mother's Day he said, "I am leaving!"

Humiliation, desperation, loneliness, hatred, and devastation blended inside my chest. Just like in a slow-motion video, I fell deep into a dark and tight hole.

What happened to all those affirmations and mantras, yoga, and subliminal messages I practiced some years back? When did I lose them and lose myself? I thought as I blamed and hated myself. *Was I worthy of his love?*

I shouted and begged God for mercy. I guess he warned me, in some way, during that nightmare, and instead of playing nice and smart I did the opposite.

I begged my future ex-boyfriend twice not to leave, but he was determined. He explained his sudden decision. While he packed his clothes he said he was not being himself with me. He said, "It has nothing to do with you. I still love you, but I should leave." A few hours later he closed the door without looking back.

I used many reasons to punish myself and didn't realize why. All the teachings and lessons Grandma had told me flooded my mind while I was in this state of misery. She introduced me to Christianity when I was very young. Therefore I got to learn about many "forbidden acts" good girls don't do. It seemed I had purposely ignored them all during my life with that man.

I was confused and didn't know what I thought. I repeated sentences like, "Yes, I know we are supposed to be obedient to God and his laws. I was disobedient. How stupid I was, and here is my punishment!"

This is when the real story begins.

Chapter One

The Undesirable Pain

Humans have around sixty thousand thoughts every day. More than half of them are memories, and the rest are the result of creativity. We all spend a good chunk of time imagining stories and events while we ignore reality. This practice is powerful and enjoyable when we use thoughts to create happiness and prosperous stories. However, most of us beautiful but naïve creatures often do the opposite. Therefore, the results are not acceptable in daily life.

John Paul II, during a papal audience on July 28, 1999, said there is no such place as hell. People must be careful in interpreting the biblical descriptions of hell, which he said are symbolic and metaphorical. The "inextinguishable fire" and "the burning oven" that the Bible speaks of "indicate the complete frustration and vacuity of a life without God," he said. In other words, *hell is a state of mind, or a state of being, not a physical or even metaphysical "place" where people who are "bad" are sent by God.*

My constant thought in my own hell was the annoying idea of weak women who fell apart easily in the midst of hard times. I saw myself as one of them and this made me hate myself even more. *I am not a stupid, sensitive woman! Come on! I learned to be confident. Didn't I?* I could not accept it if others saw me as weak.

Once I was alone I didn't want to hang out with friends anymore. *What will they think of me? What will they say about me now?* I cried.

My mind was full of images where they pointed at me, felt sorry for me, or laughed. Since that was the story I chose to believe, I also created wrong feelings about them.

Should I give up on those friends? Because they are not good friends any longer…

I realized how defensive I turned when I was on my own. I thought it was an inner strength. How confusing!

I looked back to those moments when we were still together. I told him what to do and how to think so he would depend on me and would stay with me forever. But I guess I wasn't fulfilled myself and I was dependent on him instead.

The nightmares didn't stop for many long days and nights. I lost my appetite and my desire to sleep. I pictured myself as a walking, bleeding wound.

At work I requested not to be asked anything or even looked at because I felt so sorrowful.

I looked for the best ways to liberate myself from all the self-punishment. I picked up a paper and pencil and put down all the ideas that were inside my head. Sometimes we forget how much other people suffer, some who have become inspirational people. I was motivated by them and wrote some sentences about the children who die in Africa, the economic crisis in some families, natural disasters, orphans, and so on. In the end, it didn't help at all.

I changed my mind and decided to write a letter to him.

Darling, all that you said confuses me. You told me you loved me but couldn't be in a relationship where you couldn't feel or be yourself.

You said I was the only woman in your life and unique. So I welcomed you to my home and life, and even questioned my safety as a woman.

Now you say you had business issues to solve that I didn't let you finish. Don't you think it is because you don't trust me enough to help you find out the solutions?

How about the day you said I was under your responsibility to my parents, so that you were supposed to look after us? I thought it was your promise.

How about my willingness to give up on my beliefs to follow yours? Do you really think it was worth leaving?

I also went against my values as an independent woman. I hated cooking until I met you. Since then I thought of what to prepare to satisfy you.

I invited you to join my circle of friends and my culture because I thought I came from a colorful country. I thought you had a good time but it made you uncomfortable. Don't you see the beautiful life we had built, even though in the beginning we were just two strangers?

As for the comment I made about us sealing our love, I promise not to speak about marriage again.

Our furry baby, Sophie, also misses you as much as her momma. If you said you really love, believe that LOVE will save us, because I already believe so! Let God help us solve this mess, but stay with me.

And if after this letter, you really want to leave, then do it when there is no more love. So then I'll find reasons to be apart.

I will love you forever. Your Carolita

I never delivered the letter.

Dear reader, please understand. I do not intend to blame my grandma for her teachings, my religion, or my ex-boyfriend. That sorrow has remained in the past.

After I cleared my mind a new understanding arose. It was never them; it was always me!

Because we humans are super-powerful creatures, one of our powers is the freedom of choice. We choose to believe, we choose to act, we choose to create, and we choose to feel.

And this story was a mere choice of mine.

My favorite meditation spot overlooking
the bridge to Hong Kong.

CHAPTER TWO

The Miracle

Physical activity is the best way to heal the soul and the body.

In my school days, I was likely to get sick before PE class. When the teacher mentioned the five-kilometer run, a sudden cold sweat and a tremble ran throughout my limbs. Perhaps my mood caused my body to develop symptoms or my mind commanded my body. I am not sure, but I am sure I hated running.

The story changed when I arrived in China and had yet to make any friends. I was easily bored. All the TV channels were in Chinese. My neighbors liked quietness, so loud music wasn't welcome. *Google*, *Facebook*, and other social networks were banned in the country. I ate greasy noodles almost every day.

Unexpectedly, the size of my pants that I had worn for the last ten years didn't fit me anymore. I say unexpectedly because Chinese people eat a lot each meal and they are very skinny. I thought that would apply to me as well.

Feelings of being lonely and unattractive pushed me to leave home for hours, and so I went on walks. Eventually the walks turned into runs.

After I ran for seven days for about 120 minutes, I not only lost a few pounds, but I felt happier, energetic, confident, and creative. I fell in love with running.

The passion for running is not the miracle though. Rather, it is what occurs in the mind during physical exercise.

Like many amateurs in the game of love, in the relationship with the French man I gave up on my hobbies and passions to dedicate my time to him.

On the second day of my grief, my neighbor and now good friend, Santy, pushed me to sign up for the closest gym. I agreed to go without much hesitation every day after work. I was sure this would help me overcome my sorrow since it had before.

For several evenings I cried out my pain while I ran, and wore my favorite sneakers with Sophie, the dog, by my side.

I still remember one drizzly evening while I ran through a quiet path full of bushes and cried out random questions to the sky.

"How could he give up so easily on what we had?" I shouted the same questions in different ways over and over again when something unexpected surprised me. A very tranquil voice, without any sound vibration, came to me as a message in the air and said to me, *"Have you thought that maybe it is a mere attachment of yours?"*

The silence attacked my mind and throat for a few seconds as I wondered about this, but it didn't stop my legs from jogging.

I yelled even louder this time, *"Why can't I just get what I always want?"*

"Free yourself of attachments, Carol," the voice replied. *"Only then will you be able to get what makes you happy."*

"He makes me happy!" I shouted with an upset voice.

"Does he really?"

I felt like the thing behind the voice was fooling.

"Well, fine, I am not happy now because of him, or maybe because I want to be sad. But I think I was happy being with him before. I am not really sure now," I said, shaking my head impatiently.

I didn't notice I was holding a conversation with this voice.

"So you mean he was an attachment for me? When did it happen? How?" I cried.

The voice kept quiet, but I didn't feel at peace at all, so I continued to complain. *"Fine! But if people are supposed to let everything and everyone go, why can't it be that easy? How can I let him go without feeling this pain?"*

Then the calm voice asked, *"What makes you happy?"*

"Being with him makes me happy. Well, being with someone who gives me what I think is happiness makes me happy."

"What if it is yourself?" the voice added.

"Fine, you win. I don't know where to find happiness at this point." With more arrogance, I yelled, *"Then is my pet dog an attachment as well?"*

"What makes you happy?" the voice replied.

Breathless, I stopped the run for a while, and I asked, *"Are you suggesting I should give up on him?"*

"What makes you happy?" the voice insisted.

I paused, and like a watercourse, I felt a stream of clarity run fast through my whole mind and body. *"I know I don't want him if he doesn't want me long term. So I am willing to do it now because only by setting him free would I be able to understand it all...As for my Sophie, she does make me happy. I love her, and she has been my companion."*

The message was felt in my chest this time.

"You are not alone, and you'll be provided for."

After hearing these words, a sudden stream of hope poured and washed away the uncertainty and the fear within. I fell on my knees and cried tears of joy. It was midnight, and I saw yellow flowers turn to me and felt them like a comforting hug.

Since it would take too much effort to understand where the voice had come from, I preferred to think it was the trees and flowers that had spoken. My mind was okay with associating it with the image of the old talking tree in the cartoons my sisters and I used to watch when we were kids.

Since that evening, I walked through the same bushy path every night. And the trees and the flowers still talked to me with much wisdom and love.

Dear reader, please don't think this is a supernatural event that happens to certain people. My personal belief is that we are more than a body. We are huge entities of energy with superpowers that connect us with one another and with other creatures. The key is to focus on finding that connection that provides answers to any question as well as solutions to any struggle.

In this chapter, I intend to bring awareness to the connection between the body, the mind, and the infinite source.

Recommendation 1.

Perhaps you are living a similar story with some variations. Please allow me to share the steps I took towards the enlightenment.

The recommendations you are about to learn can work well under any particular situation because they are not meant to be a first-aid kit but instead a permanent lifestyle change.

Be patient and start to work on these recommendations as the story continues.

Practice daily limb stretching and train your body at least once a day every day.

Begin with extending the arms up to the sky and hold the position for two minutes. You can also try opening the arms and pushing them backwards, so the chest is broadened. Mindfully allow this wonderful sensation to fill the whole body.

Ultimately, feel free to learn more about the brain and the effects of frequent exercise. The neural connections, development of new brain cells, and endorphins released during physical activity are nothing new. It is the best way to reduce depression, anxiety, and physical problems while also increasing memory, attention, and creativity.

Experts also say that starting with a daily walk for thirty minutes is very helpful until you figure out the particular activity you adopt as your new routine.

Let's forget for a moment about fitness and instead use the workout as an experience to release anger, pain, anxiety, and stress. You will feel lighter and more confident!

From the marketing perspective, I wonder what would happen if gyms changed their promotional campaigns from weight loss to depression loss. Would it be more attractive to their audience?

A good friend of mine told me how attractive she was to both women and men. Wherever she goes she is flawless, so people immediately notice her presence. She is a yoga teacher with the posture and confidence every woman desires.

Physical exercise not only makes you smarter and positive-minded, but also confident and naturally sexy.

This is one of the long walks Sophie and I
still enjoy together.

CHAPTER THREE

The Growth Mindset

In her book *Mindset: The New Psychology of Success,* psychologist Carol Dweck, after a decade of research, concluded that "mindset is a simple idea that makes all the difference." That was what happened to me.

It had been the longest first week on my own at home and it felt empty. The quietness bothered me from morning until dusk. I counted the days I survived the pain and the amount of times I cried.

Antonia, my friend from Russia, was incredibly busy so I missed having our "girls day" where I could share my moments and relieve my pain.

I made myself busy by stating affirmations, and one day while I searched for the old audiobooks I used to listen to I came across *The Magic* by Rhonda Byrne, the author of *The Secret*. I read her book nonstop, but I was too skeptical to follow what the book recommended. However, one evening after work I sat my butt down and worked on the grateful list the book teaches.

My head couldn't come up with anything that I was happy with or even blessed to have, as the author mentions. An unusual cold sweat covered my skin and reminded me of the day I was introduced to this new doctrine of positive thinking.

When I was twenty-two years old in my home country of Ecuador and hungry for a better level of spirituality, I asked my friend Aline to take me to the ultimate sensei she saw. I was inexplicably nervous before the first session. She said this guy could read energy, personality, and spirituality. I guess exposing all my weaknesses put me in an unpleasant state, so unconsciously I let uncertainty take over me.

I stepped into the tiny room separated from the rest of his living room by a black curtain, which he had improvised so that he could attend to his usual clients.

I extended my sweaty hand to greet the master, and after a few questions and a thirty-minute chat he could tell the lack of self-love and confidence I had, although he never said so in those specific words. But later on I got to understand the why of his advice. At the end of the session, he said, "You are different, you are special."

I did not understand his words much and stared at him while he pulled out three CDs and said, "You will listen to them three times a day and come back in a week."

The CDs were the recordings of Louise Hay who talked about her story and how affirmations freed her from cancer. That was my first time I connected to my inner goddess, divinity, or soul. Eventually I got to learn about Les Brown, Eric Thomas, Tony Robbins, Lisa Nichols, and others. They became my breakfast, lunch, and dinner.

The motivational videos and audios I found on *YouTube* helped me to decrease the level of anxiety from a ten to a three.

When I chose to change the concept or idea about myself, I arose.

Four weeks after the black Sunday I could stand on my feet every morning and go through a new, beautiful routine. Summer was around the corner, and I was able to welcome the sunlight on my windows. I faced the sea with arms wide open and had more than five reasons to thank the creator.

Happiness was home.

I enjoyed the bike rides around the bay, listened to the waves singing, and enjoyed the company of furry Sophie.

The workout at the gym with my friendly neighbor continued. On the way to the gym, Santi advised me about getting over breakups. From his male point of view, he said that my official ex-boyfriend would ask me back sometime soon because he was just confused.

My ex-boyfriend didn't act like those average new, single guys who proclaim their recent freedom and availability. He decided to torture himself and slept on the floor of his office and tried to figure out something that could save him from the crisis that had brought him to this point. I decided not to expect much as I was still sensitive.

Every evening I played subliminal audios at bedtime. This helped me sleep three hours more than I slept the previous weeks.

I was more in control of my emotions and my future.

Recommendation 2.

If you are going through any similar disappointment, I strongly suggest you work on your mind as much as you can.

It is important to *stop blaming external people* or circumstances for your particular awful situation.

Life doesn't happen to you; it happens for you!

In time you will realize how liberated you become when this pain makes sense in your life.

Search for the authors I previously mentioned and decide what suits you best according to your particular struggle.

For a speedy recovery play positive and motivational audios throughout the day and even while you sleep.

Your brain, like any muscle in your limbs, can be worked out and even change its shape.

Several studies about the science of positive thinking began with simple experiments that exposed separated groups to either photography or videos that described emotions.

Group A was shown images of happy people, love, and joy, while Group B was exposed to sadness, fear, and anger. The people in Group A showed a 19 percent increase in their moods while the people in Group B showed body sickness.

A heart made out of shadows from the surrounding trees during a bike ride.

CHAPTER FOUR

Taking Back Control

It's July and the heat is uncomfortable for most of Shekou's residents, except for me. Light and colorful dresses are my favorite choice during this season.

Shekou is a small town in the district of Nanshan and the majority of expats live here. In the summer it feels like a permanent holiday. There are many Western food restaurants, open swimming pools, exciting nightlife, bars with live music, and all of this by the bay.

I was concerned about this summer break since I would be on my own for longer periods of time. I kept my mind busy after work for weeks, so when I wasn't at work I thought it would be difficult.

Mom thought it would be a good idea to be my companion. I didn't know whether her visit would be helpful or not because when I felt blue I wanted to be alone. I agreed to host her and her husband. They both flew from the US to visit China for the first time.

It was the hottest summer registered in forty years, and my mindlessness was at its peak during their stay with me. I still feel bad about it because after they traveled around Beijing, Hong Kong, and Shenzhen for two weeks they left China with a bitter taste in their mouths.

I drove back home after I dropped them off at the airport. I was back home and alone.

When I got home I watched the sunset and received a weblink from Antonia that contained several testimonials of people who dealt with the same situation I was going through. The link was a collection of stories of miracles after people had practiced the mental visualization and law of attraction.

I read a few and came across this one lady who described a very similar story. She visualized a reunion with her love interest, and that is what happened. She not only imagined that he was there with her, but also pretended he was physically present and placed two sets of dishes and the nicest cutlery on the table every night before dinner. She also slept on one side of the bed and imagined him on the other side.

At the end of the testimonial he had contacted her and invited her to spend Christmas at his house in the mountains.

Wow! I thought to myself. There was hope he would be back. But did I want him back?

At this point I was still confused. But in the end I followed the woman's methods from the story and I set two plates, left one side of the wardrobe for his clothes, and slept on one side of the bed.

Soon he came home sometimes to hang out with Sophie. He said he missed her. I found these visits as signs we would be back together someday, so I continued the strategy the blog had suggested.

Thirty Years Old

It was about to be my thirtieth birthday, and like every girl I expected it to be unforgettable.

One night, days before my celebration, he surprised me at home with his latest recipe of gratin dauphinoise. Over the meal I warned him about my birthday and my wish for a romantic dinner.

Before I spoke to him, I had read advice on another blog that explained the best way to deal with the "memory lapse" men sometimes suffer. The female author suggested, "Kindly let your man know about that special date a couple of weeks before." It also suggested to do it two or three times within the same period. It sounded convenient to me, so I did it.

He apparently heard me say, "I'd like to have a good day on my birthday because the thirtieth birthday is usually a memorable day."

The night before the big day I heard he was on a short business trip and got delayed on the way back. He'd suddenly felt so sick that he stayed overnight at the house of one of his married friends in that town. I cried before I finished reading his message, because I knew in my heart he wouldn't spend time with me on this special day.

The punch hit me in the lower part of the stomach. I was disappointed and tired of the same thing over and over again. I didn't sleep that night as I thought of ways to finally keep myself apart from him. Did I trip on the same stone again? Maybe…

On the morning of my birthday I hung out in the perfect sixty-four m2 apartment with a wide sea view, where I lived the last nine months.

After 11 a.m. I took a shower and pampered myself. I picked my wallet, a book, my favorite lipstick, some menthols, my passport, and departure form and put them all inside my dress bag.

I rushed to the closest border to Hong Kong and took the first bus to the main island where there is a snobby bar area.

I walked around for a while, and after fifteen months of not smoking, I bought a box of those thin cigarettes that smoking girls usually like.

I sat on an empty barstool and ordered a mojito. The bartender acknowledged me. It was happy hour, so I had a second drink for free. I sat there and sipped the cocktail and pretended to read my book to distract the tears and to avoid the stares of people who passed by.

Four hours later, and with six glasses of white rum with mint and hierba buena in me, my phone rang. It was him. He apologized and asked me to meet him at home. I was too far from home. I wanted him to come after me. So, I hung up. I paid the bill and tipsily walked to the bus station to go home. It grew dark quickly, and when I opened the door to my home, I found a big bouquet of red roses without any note.

I grabbed my diary and pencil before I even changed my clothes. I was about to write a serious commitment to myself. *Don't EVER let your best moments depend on someone else.*

Right after I highlighted that statement, this clear thought caught me: It is not him; it is not the situation. It is me! I am the only person responsible for this life.

I take full control of my life from now on!

With the help of my new Surface Pro, I researched a good plan for the next semester. I heard the beep of the chat on my phone. It was an advertisement that requested speakers to perform in the largest community in China that was managed by an American guy and his Chinese future ex-girlfriend. Huh! What a coincidence!

Whatever! I thought.

I clicked on the link, went over the requirements, and applied. Yes, I did it!

The next morning a message waited for me. I was selected to speak to three hundred-plus attendees. Yeah, yeah, yeah!

Recommendation 3.

It is very easy to judge people and blame them for everything we go through.

I strongly suggest not to look for villains because you won't see the opportunities and uncover the wisdom within.

Take more time to decide the kind of job, partner, family, trip, or friends you want for your life. Act as if you have them now and create the feeling that sticks to you until they knock at your door.

Understand that if you take control of your ship you have more chances to get what you really want.

An extra suggestion—something that I did for a full week that helped me reunite with my inner strength—is to convince yourself you are in charge by repeating this statement several times:

This is my 'Spaceship' and I drive it wherever makes me happy!

I decide to make my own decisions based on what is best for me.

I decide what is best for me.

Feel free to make your own affirmations based on your specific situation. Don't forget that the longer the time of your daily repetitions, the more effective and immediate the results.

This image shows some of the feedback from readers after every article that was published in the local newspaper.

CHAPTER FIVE

Life Purpose

I went for a walk with Sophie and sat down under a long bridge on a rock that faced the sea. On one side was beautiful Shenzhen where I lived for the last six years and on the other side was my unrequited love, the vibrant Hong Kong.

I remembered the very first time I stood on Shenzhen's soil—the breeze blew through my thick hair while my skin was in ecstasy under the humidity in this part of Asia. I smiled to the wind and thought how far I had gone, even against my parents' will. I remembered when my dad spoke angrily about my decision to migrate far from home while my younger sister defended my opportunity to move to China.

Some people called me crazy; others called me brave. Either way, I saw myself the same as anyone else with struggles, mistakes, and achievements.

I came from a middle-class family where money was an uncomfortable member without further explanations; Dad was just afraid of not having enough.

As children, whenever my sisters and I asked for a new toy or ice cream, Dad was very direct and firm: "We can't afford it, sweetie." This was his usual explanation when our requests were denied.

I can't blame him; he was one of eleven siblings whose father and sick mother couldn't provide.

My dear mother was a woman with many adopted and personal insecurities who did the best she could and followed my dad wherever he went.

My parents tried their best to provide for us, but they didn't say they loved their choices in life. Probably because they both had one thing in common, responsibility, which I define as the ability to respond to one's current situation. My parents indeed lived up to this definition.

My sisters and I were their responsibility and they responded accordingly and forgot to fulfill their own needs as individuals (what should have been their priority) and as a couple (what should have come second). My parents were not the only ones who lived this way. Many of our parents came from the generation where you were supposed to study, get a good job, have a family and provide, retire and … this was how it was for the rest of their lives. They weren't taught to pursue things they enjoyed or to follow their passions. That was for hippies, not for serious people. I will always admire the very serious man my dad was.

After my first speaking gig one Thursday in autumn, I was invited to speak at other events and places. That was the beginning of a promising career.

It was a bit less than six months since my breakup occurred and I went from zero to my own hero.

I missed my ex-boyfriend less, my body was toned, and my mind was aware.

I have a purpose now! I thought.

My dream was to speak to thousands of people and pass the message of the incredible life that comes after a deep crisis.

I am not an English speaker; I am not a Chinese speaker. I don't have a company registered yet, and I don't have a degree in coaching. But I intend to be an inspiration to humanity. I am ready to make my dad proud (who ultimately supported my idea of living in China as a motivational speaker and coach).

Regardless of the unknown,
I am going to make it!

It was another day full of opportunities, and I practiced my lines for a new event later that night. I chose the best dress and hairstyle. With Sophie as my audience, I rehearsed in front of the mirror for the last time. The venue was a little less than an hour away from home. I decided to leave early so I wouldn't be sweaty by the time I arrived. The host had been waiting, and with a bottle of water in hand, he welcomed me.

The show began, and I was invited to the stage. After the first five minutes of my presentation, an unexpected guest showed up.

It was him—the reason for the pain that would become the inspiration to uncover the best version of me.

Recommendation 4.

In the last ten years we have been exposed to the message "live for your passions." It is a very good marketing campaign and it is very meaningful to me. When I finally live the entrepreneurial lifestyle (to live by the beach, travel when I can, and work from my computer) I'll know that it is possible to live a dream. *Only when you know your dream.*

Until you explore your passions, abilities, and dreams, you won't be able to live in a way different from your current situation.

In this chapter I encourage you to spend a good chunk of time every day and read, listen, and take notes of all those things you enjoy the most.

Expose yourself to new environments, volunteer, and let your new abilities flow so you meet the other side of yourself.

This new task may take some time. Set an eighteen-month goal to dip into your life's purpose. Be aware of the needed length of time and embrace patience and hope.

Please remain kind to yourself. It can be challenging as well. You may be halfway towards a goal your parents, spouse/family, or mentors set for you. I do know it is easy to give up at any time.

Please don't take any actions or make choices until you are sure of that potential life purpose.

When you have found it, trust that the universe will take over from there.

One of the wonderful speaking gigs in Shenzhen.

CHAPTER SIX

The Power of Meditation

Once I became more involved in the entrepreneurial community, I attended to business and networked here and there, which helped me develop more confidence.

I actually had my moment of fame in town and I loved it. New connections, new ideas, and new little opportunities to strategic partnerships emerged.

I took Antonia with me to one of those wine and networking events, and afterwards we agreed she'd stay at my place because I was about to try her ultimate ritual: "The Meditation."

We chatted about it a few times before that night, but I was not interested at all. I thought it would be too complicated and difficult to completely shut off the mind and remain silent for long periods of time. I agreed to do it because she insisted and, since she was my best friend, I thought the main rule of a BFF was to fully appreciate the other's choices.

After we walked Sophie for some time and returned home, we sat down on the long mat on the floor of the living room with some lighted candles around us.

Antonia played some Taoist music with some chants in the background, and she instructed me to focus on only the music.

I closed my eyes and encouraged myself to follow her requests. Then a strange movie played in my mind. There was a rocky desert with small men in red who sang, and my body was like a statue made of elastic mud. My spine extended greatly, and I could see my neck and head in a couple of imaginary hands that molded them in different shapes.

Later on, this mud was gone, and instead, a very bright ball of light with a long tail appeared and bounced from one side to another at such a high speed that I barely could follow. I understood the ball was me; it didn't have a head or eyes, nor even a smiley mouth, but I knew with certainty that thing was full of joy and excitement.

Then I was back to the dry place with those singing men in red. I heard Antonia hardly breathe and she rubbed her feet, so I understood that was the moment to finish the session. I opened my eyes even before I wanted to. The state of joy and peace I experienced during the trance was delightful.

We discussed our visions, and, to my surprise, I discovered that we had both seen pretty much the same thing.

I suddenly knew I would add the meditation to my morning routine.

From that point on, right after I wake up, I began to meditate for twenty-five minutes. Then I listened to audios and motivational speeches. Afterward, I read *The Power* by Rhonda Byrne followed by the affirmations while I held the winner posture for two or three minutes.

I was so fascinated with this new form of meditation that I not only practiced it in the morning but after work as well. I couldn't wait to come back home and do it as many times as my butt would let me, because eventually it grew sore.

More opportunities arose due to my fame in town and great connections in the networking events. I successfully wrote daily articles for a column of the local newspaper because readers adopted my message as their morning motivation while they traveled to work. The list of followers grew to 1,500 within a month.

My mind worked faster and more creatively while I developed the title and content for the upcoming day's article as well as other ideas that would bring me a step closer to my goal of becoming a Life Coach.

I decided to take a part-time job while I made sure I had enough time to work on my new dream job.

After work I had a light dinner, and afterward I sat for another thirty-minute meditation and then went to the gym.

One day, my ex-boyfriend called to get my opinion about a Landmark forum he was invited to attend for a second time. Earlier we had traveled to Hong Kong to participate in the introductory presentation. After he saw me on stage a few times as I motivated people and told my story, he thought the forum would be a good tool for me to improve my skills. I didn't feel that way, so I declined.

He wanted to know my opinion if he took part in the program instead. He said he was confused himself. So I persuaded him to take action and attend. The Monday after the two-day intensive course, he discussed the breakthrough he experienced, and to my surprise, he admitted he had some issues that stopped him from enjoying his life.

Something equal to a big stream welled up inside my chest. I realized how much I loved that man, not only because of his constant sense of humor, but because of his enthusiasm to fix his life.

I was so fascinated by this process that began when I adopted individualism as my new lifestyle. I didn't blame him anymore and I even gave up on the idea of his return.

Recommendation 5.

No matter how hard your crisis knocks you down, a mindful focus is the only way to bring yourself to the oasis of peace and love when the war happens outside. Please consider meditation as a main factor to cover yourself in peace and clarity.

YouTube offers many good video guides for beginner, intermediate, or advanced practitioners. For guided meditation, my favorite one is the "Honest Guys."

If you are a skeptic as I was, I invite you to learn more about the numerous benefits of meditation from reliable sources.

This may sound cliché, but it makes a lot of sense: just let it be.

Let your focus be on yourself, your goals, and your plan of action. Then the tools, as well as the people you need around you, will surely become the pieces that will fall into the right place because that is the unchangeable law of gravity.

The *Shenzhen Daily* published an article about me on
Monday 11, 2016. It was printed on the second page.

CHAPTER SEVEN

Trust!

Unlike Shanghai, Shenzhen is a city that provides a more mature home for families and retired foreigners all around China.

In my small town of Shekou, a community of expatriates and business owners created weekly meet-up sessions during lunch to network and look for ways to cooperate with each other and new members.

I signed up to join and met a Colombian, Ricky Cortez, in one of the meetings. He ran a mentoring program that encouraged individuals to become entrepreneurs. He believed they could profit by turning their passions into a business.

I had heard of him even before that encounter. An incredible Israeli man attended my first talk and was so delighted by my story that he invited me to be part of the first community of personal developers in town. He said he was in touch with another man like me whose name was Ricky. Through this coincidental encounter, the three of us could join forces, where we could bring solutions to the community.

Eventually, we held meetings with ten other people who served on the same field—great men and fewer local women, which made me the only international female mentor among them—and we did as well as we could.

I found it fascinating how speedy this new beginning unfolded. I was a part of my first but yet favorite mastermind group with Meir (the Israeli) and Ricky. I liked to call them my elder brothers. They clearly knew how to support and guide me well.

As I meditated over the events, I pictured myself as Alice in Wonderland who stood at the closed doors, curious and hesitant about what door to open first. When she opened one it took her to a different and surreal world. Perhaps *this* was my door. When I opened it everything else was provided, until this fantasy distracted me from the upcoming breakdown.

A large group of achievers was in town, and I was excited to network with new and potential private mentees. I put on my best executive outfit and planned to be there until the end of the five-hour event.

In the middle of the show my phone rang. It was the landlady, who rudely told me to leave the apartment.

I felt so stupid because after all this progress in my life, I thought I was finally ready to take care of myself. *How come I forgot about this simple, basic need?* I wondered and punished myself again.

I had become so involved in this new reality that I'd forgotten about the deadline to sign the apartment's leasing contract. I didn't worry about the bills because my ex-boyfriend said he would continue to take care of the bills for the fantastic apartment which we had called our love nest.

I broke into tears and immediately left the conference room. I was homeless and had very little money in my bank account because the part-time job helped to cover only the very basic expenses. It was the beginning of winter and I couldn't come up with any place for Sophie and me to stay.

Desperate but convinced that I had the tools to help me find answers, I lit candles and sat down on the mat by the porch.

A twenty-minute meditation saved me one more time. I remembered the words I was told in the beginning during my run. *"You're not alone. You'll be provided for." I just needed to trust because I am a daughter of God, so I am worthy.*

As I packed my clothes, I noticed some stuff he'd left behind, so I phoned him and asked him to come by and pick up his things. An hour later he showed up. While we peacefully talked just like we used to, he asked me to move in with him.

I spoke with friends of mine and learned that most of them lived in apartments with roommates as a way to save money. Because he had asked me unexpectedly, I went to a cheap hotel for a while until I figured it out.

I couldn't tell if he'd asked me to move in with him because he missed me, he loved me, he felt guilty, or because his religion wouldn't forgive him if he let me go alone.

Perhaps my readers and followers think it would have been a huge mistake to accept his offer. Well, sorry to disappoint you because I did accept it.

I pledged to have him back, but this time I did not enjoy it at all because the December cold was felt not only outside but inside the apartment as well.

Recommendation 6.

Understand that the challenges won't ever stop whether you are prepared or not.

It is not enough to remain positive. Trust is required. Although, honestly, I still struggle with this.

Growing trust is like growing a muscle. It can only happen if you work out frequently. The best way to find trust is to combine meditation, mindfulness, and affirmation. Another important ingredient is patience. Just like the workout, more time and frequent repetitions lead to a better final product.

Regardless of your religion or doctrine, you're meant to be part of this entire community called humanity because you are a creature of energy. And since there are seven billion people in the world, statistically you have high chances to give and receive assistance because this is our main purpose on earth.

The first Influencer on social media who helped to spread
my story internationally.
Thanks, Dustin Watchman.

CHAPTER EIGHT

The Opportunity

2015 was the year of the breakup. I believe I was somehow warned but I didn't believe in the accuracy of the oriental predictions.

Before spring break of the same year while I taught kindergarten English to twenty-four two-year-olds, I got a cute teaching assistant who was very traditional Chinese. She joined me during the office time to plan for the upcoming class. When finished, we gave ourselves a short break. She asked me about my Chinese Zodiac animal. I wasn't familiar with the characteristics of the animals and their luck and said I didn't know. With her guidance we found out that I was an ox.

The next year was the Year of the Goat. We were curious about the predictions and googled it immediately.

I wrote this guide to moving on twelve months after the end of the Year of the Goat. Therefore, unlike the Year of the Rooster (Jan. 28, 2017 – Feb. 15, 2018) the goat would bring intense events that would end in disaster and calamity for most of the animals including mine. The prediction was that relationships might end up in a happy marriage or a tragic breakup.

My romance was perfect, so the first option sounded more accurate because I had been lucky my whole life. At least that is what I always preferred to believe. But a happy marriage didn't happen to me. Otherwise this story wouldn't be mine and this book wouldn't exist.

I was back in the new house with him. Christmastime had never been more bitter than that one. I refused to continue to work as a schoolteacher because I had better plans for my life. I acted like a spoiled girl and skyped my mom in Aurora, Colorado, to ask her to let me stay in her place for a few weeks until I figured something out. As most loving mothers, she couldn't contain her joy and quickly approved it.

I booked the flight for mid-January, right before the end of the Chinese New Year of the "evil goat." I tried to keep my mind busy and positive while I stayed at his new home.

While I worked on my talks and networking, a good friend of mine had referred my speaking services to an Australian and senior NLP coach who had built a huge and active community of self-development searchers in Shanghai for about ten years.

I was excited to connect with him over traditional Chinese social media, but instead I held a long conversation with him by phone. As another stroke of luck, the call ended with a new arrangement for me to speak in Shanghai before my trip to the US.

It was the first time I flew to the popular city of Shanghai. So I bet you can tell where the rocket of happiness took me that night.

There were two weeks to go until the big event in Shanghai and I thought of some topics to talk about. In silence, I summarized the high peaks and the dark bottoms this adventure was dragging me into so I could find the best message that would interest my new audience. But I realized there was something that bothered me in my gut that affected my breathing rhythm, as if I could predict the new bucket of ice I was about to receive.

I rehearsed the speech about "The Ego" over and over while on the trip to the center of the Asian Giant. I was inspired to put together readings and experiences for this event by the strong desire to let the supreme intelligence take over my struggles. Although I was supposed to speak about setting the mind free of pain and suffering, I was not sure I could train others in this area because I suffered myself.

On the day of my trip I waited at the airport for my flight. I meditated, but something stronger happened within. It felt like a heavy rock that sat in the back of my head and caused me great discomfort, something between worry and fear.

The winter was extremely cold, which contributed to my desire to not give the speech. Not only was the weather to blame, but also my gut feeling predicted an imminent disappointment.

Hey! I am about to conquer one of the most exciting Asian cities in the world. How can I give up on that? I consoled myself with these thoughts.

It was time to board. I grabbed my warm coffee and books and walked ahead to find the right aisle and seat.

Part of the deal was to stay in the Motivate Shanghai home. A student of NLP and future coach would host me there and help me arrange the event.

I followed the instructions and trusted my Chinese speaking skills. I arrived at the apartment on time and waited for the girl who would become my new best friend and angel, Henar.

I read the book *Conversations with God* for the third time in one of the rooms with the heater turned up high. Then I heard the door open and footsteps on the old, wood floor of the living room. Almost too lazy to walk out of the warm bed, I put on my slippers and stood up to introduce myself. I visualized her as a woman full of joy and light.

Since I knew she was an NLP coach-to-be, I thought I would request a couple of sessions with her. I trusted she would be able to help me feel better. But when I finally met her, I saw a sweet face soaked in tears. This was the Spanish girl, Henar.

It was an awkward situation because at that particular moment I was not in the mood to comfort a stranger.

I was still not very skilled in relationships and asked her if she wanted to be alone and meet up the day after. She insisted we talk that same evening.

We agreed to go out for some food. I tried to talk about her issue while we walked so she could free herself. Instead, she asked first. "*So, Carol, when did you find your life purpose? I mean, I know from the coaches in my circle that they found out theirs when they were going through tough times. What is your story?*" she asked.

To my surprise she was knowledgeable about the many authors and coaches I enjoyed the most.

She took me to a traditional Chinese dumplings restaurant. Over the meal, we talked as if we were old friends. After I told her my story she opened up and revealed her emotions about her job, loneliness, and her old, personal struggles.

We had a great time together the next few days as we set up this event.

When the day of the engagement arrived, there were six multinational ladies interested to hear me speak.

My speech and event could have been a blast if only I hadn't learned about the secret trip he, my bedmate, had planned. He flew to Thailand to celebrate his good friend's birthday with several single and available Thai ladies.

At that moment all those emotions weeks before and at the airport made sense.

I cried all night prior to the big event.

Recommendation 7.

Although things weren't going well for me, I am glad I didn't give up on the great opportunity to reach Shanghai and get in touch with the pioneers of the personal development community there. My career got a big boost because I did it once and would eventually do it three more times.

Here is my recommendation. If you are learning about yourself and your life purpose, I strongly suggest you dare to catch new opportunities when they come.

First of all it can offer you a whole new spectrum of opportunities. And secondly, you may develop new skills or sharpen old ones that will be needed in future bigger projects.

Go against your fears!

Life is made of thousands of opportunities presented when you are ready to work on your passions. Dare to pick them wisely and don't hesitate to milk them while you can.

The night before our first event. Henar and I after a great NLP session. My eyes are tired of crying.

CHAPTER NINE

The Last Shot in the Year of the Goat

Thirty-five hours split between three different planes finally brought me to the other side of the Pacific Ocean where my mom and elder brother expected my arrival.

I carried a light suitcase because I didn't plan to stay a long time away from the promising land of opportunities.

But guess what?

I found more opportunities this time in America and I didn't question saying *yes* to them. The few pieces of clothing I packed were not enough for my unplanned four months in Colorado.

Before the end of the Year of the Goat I found the best word to describe the entire year: roller-coaster.

It took me sharply to very high peaks of excitement and happiness and very deep dips of misery and sadness. But in the end I can say I am grateful. Because when the maturity, wisdom, and knowledge found me, they introduced me to the new woman who emerged in me.

Right before the end of the twelve months of the lunar calendar and the latest disappointment back in China, the naughty goat was about to pull the trigger one last time to hit me with its best shot.

The second night at the Cline's (Mom's and her husband's) cozy home, Mom and I caught up over a cup of hot chamomile tea. I had slept the whole day, so I was energetic enough to talk about my breakthroughs and discoveries the rest of the night.

It was close to midnight and we still sat at the table. I was delighted to tell her the great technique this guy named Tony Robbins used to heal millions of people around the world. Mom's eyes were tired but wide open as she listened and saw my excitement. Suddenly, she looked at her laptop and the name of the guy I just mentioned was written on a promo banner of her *Facebook* wall. With her warm hands, she turned the screen to me and wondered if the guy on her screen was the same person I had just named.

A big "Wow!" came out of me.

I quickly closed my eyes and placed my hands on my face, my unique way to express explosive excitement. I said, "I would do anything to get a ticket to see this man speak if he were in town."

Mom read aloud that within the next two days the 2016 Congress of Achievers was scheduled to happen in Denver, Colorado. There were eight speakers, and Tony Robbins was the last one.

What? I was shocked. Another miracle just happened to me.

I hustled to contact Antonia back in China to borrow some money to attend the event.

Mom's husband drove their old, blue Corolla that they'd bought from my sister-in-law fast on the way to the Convention and Exhibition Center in Colorado. Stepfather, Mother, and I searched for a specific gate to the Bellco theater. I guessed the right door and got out of the car.

Mom handed me a lunchbox with some snacks and I felt like a little girl on her first day of school.

I was nervous and insecure because despite my English skills I found it difficult to understand some Americans, especially when I felt out of my comfort zone.

I spotted the counter and held my ticket that showed the seat I'd booked online in case they couldn't find my name on the list. I stood in line. I watched attentively and followed people's movements to imitate them so I wouldn't look like a confused foreigner.

It was my turn, and they asked for my name and seat. I said, "Carol Zurita, Ruby Seat."

I'd bought the cheapest ticket online. I didn't care if I was far from the stage as long as I could be inside.

I showed the scan code on my phone; they verified it and placed a paper band around my wrist. "Diamond Seat" was written on it.

"Huh?" I exclaimed.

Surprised, I looked back to the guy and he said, "Your seat wasn't Ruby."

At this point, I was not only scared but also confused because of the new seat. I walked inside the partially empty theater full of labels and signs. I tried to find out where the guy from the counter sent me. I passed through the hall from the bottom of the theater when I saw the Ruby seating area, but ten meters ahead showed Diamond.

"What?" I cried.

I was right behind the Platinum and the VIP seats.

The unexpected happened. I was only twelve seats away from the stage!

Bells sounded in my head. I was so blessed, and I loved it.

"I am not taking it for granted!" I said quietly with my eyes to the ceiling.

Amen!

Recommendation 8.

Now that you have read the previous chapters, hopefully you agree with me that any mess in life can be fixed when the inner game changes. But to bring clarity to your life, you must look for guidance in people with the ability and passion to do it. Many mentors are out there; life coaches, authors, speakers, yogis, and others who have devoted their lives to save others. So learn to invest in yourself!

It's necessary to dedicate time, funds, and willingness to attend events like these. But personal development is just as serious of a business as financial services or health services are. Don't let the comments of "how expensive the events are" and "how much they take advantage of you" drive you.

You may hear different opinions about this industry. There are fake doctors, fake priests, fake sellers, and fake coaches. I learn more about the coach and search for free content before I pay for a book or speaking engagement.

Visualize your beliefs and struggles as a white light on one side of a prism. The prism itself is the coaches, masters, books, and audios. When the prism is exposed to the white light, then a rainbow is projected to the other side. Let the prism project a colorful new life for you.

To let this happen keep yourself humble and open to accept new concepts about life.

At the Unstoppable event 2016. I am excited to see
Tony Robbins for the very first time.

CHAPTER TEN

Sealing the Past

At the event I remembered the words of Henaras as I listened to the first few speakers and their inspirational stories: "Coaches discovered their life purpose out of the middle of their crisis."

Lisa Nichols shared the promise she made to her newborn baby when she couldn't afford a package of twelve-dollar Pampers and had to use a towel to roll the little boy in.

I felt touched and motivated to keep rowing my boat despite the waters.

During break time, shyness and jet lag kept me away from the friendly people who were already socializing. I am not usually shy; however, I was in a country I barely understood. I had been in the Asian bubble for so long that

I almost forgot how to interact in the western side of the globe. I also didn't have any common topic to start a conversation.

I was only a third of the way through what the program offered and yet I was mesmerized and dreamed of myself being on stage and telling my story to thousands of people.

I was satisfied with my seating arrangement and almost wanted to skip the bathroom break.

I ate all my snacks before the speakers came up to the stage so I could have both hands to take notes and participate.

Gerry Robert, the next speaker, talked about how he became rich by publishing a book. I was very curious about his speech because I had an interest in writing a book someday.

He told many good jokes in the middle of his speech. I was fascinated with his enthusiasm and energy. He seemed to know the tricks needed to sell and market any product.

That woke up the sleeping giant in me to recover all my skills in marketing and business. I majored in international marketing in college because I was hooked from the very first class I took in that field.

Mr. Robert invited everyone to sign up for the upcoming boot camp in town. At this camp, attendees would learn how to write a book in forty-eight hours, fund it, and of course, grow rich. The price was less than a hundred dollars. He made it sound pretty cheap. But I didn't have that money. Instead of feeling down I reminded myself that I was supposed to trust, so I distracted my eyes by reading the biography of the final but well-expected speaker.

The transition between speakers was longer this time, so I took advantage of it and rushed to the restroom so I wouldn't miss Tony Robbins' talk.

I fixed the wrinkles of my sweater in front of the mirror so the phrase stamped on it could be seen clearly. It said *TODAY, I AM FEELING FANTASTIC!* My name and logo were listed below. This is one of the quotes I had proudly created and stamped on summer T-shirts and winter sweaters to sell.

I ran back to my seat, and I could see the theater was fully booked and there were more people than chairs. I guess there were a lot of people that bought a ticket just to see Tony, not the other speakers.

I felt blessed one more time!

The host rallied the audience when he finally announced the next speaker, and the euphoria began.

The wonderful six-foot-seven-inch Tony Robbins arrived to the stage. He discussed common excuses people made that stopped them from achieving what they really wanted.

He asked volunteers to take the microphone and share their particular struggles so he could help them find a solution by applying his unique techniques.

A few brave ones took the microphone and shared their personal experiences. Just like me, they knew they would be able to learn how to drive their boat to become a solution maker for others with similar struggles.

A beautiful refugee from Syria stood up and spoke about her horrible story as a bomb victim. All she wanted was to find the right tools and build a better platform that could assist more people in similar conditions. With a very simple and straightforward message, Tony let her know that the empowerment and tools may be found within.

His exceptional performance mixed with powerful music and colorful lights brought us to freely sing, shout, cry, jump, shake, and hug strangers.

We experienced the climax of life. As this intense session of breakthroughs continued, I sensed something within my ribs, as if I was ready to welcome the new!

It was time to let the giant come out and take control from that day on.

Recommendation 9.

Don't play the victim game!

From my story you might blame my ex because he left home unexpectedly. I blamed him too until I realized that I played the victim by blaming him.

I invite you to create your own reality and don't blame others or let them make choices for you.

Define your path and sharpen your tools. Bring the people and the resources to you. *Do not* blame others for failure. Take responsibility because you picked them as your allies. Learn the lesson, and ultimately try something different again!

Understand that this path is a process with varying levels of difficulty, just like when a child learns to ride a bike. His first bike may have three wheels for better balance. Then one is removed but it is low enough, so the child can use his feet to maintain control. Eventually, the bike is slimmer and higher, and the child learns to race up and down hills.

Another example is when you learn a new language. You may begin with very basic words. Later on you may form sentences. At last you may hold full conversations with native speakers.

It is all a process. It just takes time and dedication, but most importantly, *it can only happen if you take the step to make it happen.*

Here I wait for my brother who did the photo shoot for the cover of my first book.

CHAPTER ELEVEN

I Am Not Chinese!

I sat at the table in my parents' place, ready for dinner and for prayers, and the only thing on my mind was to thank God for the enlightenment and breakthroughs that came from the Tony Robbins event. It was officially the best day of my life.

I felt so fulfilled and ready to define my next steps. Words burst out of my mind.

I'll take part in the book-writing boot camp!

Mom didn't think it was a good idea. But I was convinced I would do what was necessary to make it a reality.

At last I did sign up and showed up to the first day of boot camp.

Since I was not an American citizen, I didn't own credit cards, so I carried cash with me and trusted they would accept it like in the old days.

My mom handed me a paper bag with a sandwich and some fruit for lunch. This time her husband drove me to the event venue.

I was committed to network and connect with fresh minds and wore my most confident outfit. I walked into the reception area.

"Hi, I come from China," I said. "But I am not Chinese."

This part of the story was always tricky to explain.

Should I say that…I just lived there as a result of an impulsive desire to run away and stayed longer than planned and…? Nah! I said to myself. I didn't want to bore them with my words. Instead, I said, "I am not a citizen, *but* not an illegal either. So I have only cash to pay for this event."

The person in charge wasn't comfortable with the money, so he called someone else for approval. But it was too early in the day and the full team hadn't arrived yet.

Instead he signed me up and posted a note so he could remind me to pay later. I was happy because I could still be in the conference room.

I chose a chair in the middle of the crowd so this time I could let my social skills flow. I couldn't wait to have neighbors so I could start a conversation.

A lovely lady sat at my right side and greeted me. I said, "Hi...and welcome."

She smiled and said, "Welcome to you too. Have fun!"

We chatted, and I told my story about Asia. To my surprise, she was amazed. When the host jumped on the stage and asked the audience to raise their hands if they were visitors who were in town for the occasion, my friendly companion pulled my arm and forced me to energetically wave high. The host saw me and asked me to stand up and loudly introduce myself.

"My name is Carol, and I come from China, *but I am not Chinese.*"

Again, the tricky part of explaining that, I thought to myself.

The man at the microphone asked for my nationality and full name.

I forgot that in America you introduce yourself by stating your full name. In China names are pretty short, so I'd learned to skip my last name to avoid confusing the locals.

"Carol Zurita from Ecuador," I said.

Numerous people turned their heads curiously and probably thought this was strange.

There were hundreds of people in the room, so the host moved on to someone else, and I felt like a star.

Out of my backpack I pulled my water bottle, pencils, colored pens, and the pink, blank notebook Mom had handed me the night before because she noticed I had nothing decent to write my notes on.

I was embarrassed because since I arrived a week ago, although I was thirty, I had been treated like a ten-year-old. But hey! It is always good to be spoiled sometimes.

This was a very interesting experience/experiment to test my level of self-confidence. Although I consider myself to be an extrovert, for years when I visited the US, shame and fear of being bullied because of my accent or for not being a white person was always in the back of my head.

While these insecurities wandered in my mind, I dared to speak up to hundreds of people and, to my surprise, I was inspirational and brave to some attendees. They found me interesting because I originally came from the very small and poor country of Ecuador, traveled to the other side of the world, and survived it despite the lack of resources.

The lesson of just accepting myself as I am is greater than my ego because *I am great being myself with my choices.*

Recommendation 10.

Many believe in "fake it until you make it." I believe in building yourself and being yourself.

I can only suggest you invest a lot of time in yourself.

Make weekly or monthly breaks and find quiet places for yourself.

Ask yourself questions every day for two or three hours. Explore your thoughts and memories. The brain is designed to give answers, but clear and straightforward questions must be asked first.

When you are alone let go of the shame and reveal the emotions. Then imagine them as a character. Give them a name, face, size, and even colors. Talk to them as if they were friends of yours. Let them leave if they cause you discomfort. And to the ones that feel good, thank them and explain to them how much you love them.

This simple exercise may help you recover your confidence, and soon you will discover how your power takes over your mind and body.

Finally, I invite you all to jump into the boat of opportunities and believe that you have a great potential. Know there are many others who are ready and willing to join you, serve you, and help you take over the world!

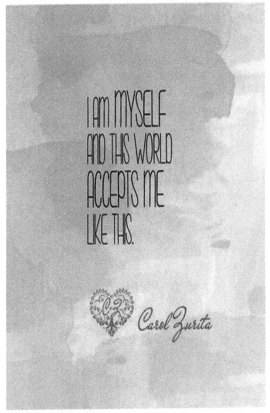

One of the quotes I made for the T-shirts I sold online.

ABOUT THE AUTHOR

Carol Zurita, origi-
nally from Ecuador began
her career as a motiva-
tional speaker in China
right after a devastating
break up.

After a few talks to
small audiences and with
an unexpected massive positive feedback.

She would begin writing daily articles that
people made their morning happy reading.

Eventually she would appear in local
newspapers and TV stations.

Still, dealing with her recent broken
heart her popularity helped the recovery and
ultimately, she would write her book.

The purpose of the book is to empower
other people who go through hard times and
become unstoppable and unbreakable.